Contents

(continued on the next page)

✳ This activity includes a reproducible.

✳ This activity includes a reproducible.

SCHOLASTIC

50+ Super-Fun Math Activities

by Jennifer Nichols

NEW YORK • TORONTO • LONDON • AUCKLAND • SYDNEY
MEXICO CITY • NEW DELHI • HONG KONG • BUENOS AIRES

Teaching Resources

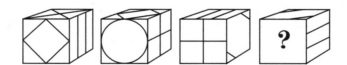

Edited by Jean Liccione

Cover design by Ka-Yeon Kim-Li

Interior design by Ellen Matlach Hassell for Boultinghouse & Boultinghouse, Inc.

Interior illustrations by Maxie Chambliss and Manuel Rivera

ISBN-13: 978-0-545-20821-5

ISBN-10: 0-545-20821-1

2 3 4 5 6 7 8 9 10   40   17 16 15 14 13 12 11 10

Introduction

Welcome to *50+ Super-Fun Math Activities: Grade 6*. This book contains a unique collection of activities that reinforce important first-grade-level mathematics concepts and skills and support the math standards recommended by the National Council of Teachers of Mathematics (NCTM). See page 6, for more.

The book is organized by nine major content topics. When you're teaching a particular math concept or skill, just check the Contents page. Browse the activities listed under each topic to find just the right one to reinforce students' learning. Each major topic has projects, games, activities, and ready-to-use reproducibles designed to reinforce specific learning objectives. The activities will also get students interested and excited, and encourage them to value math and become confident mathematicians.

ACTIVITY FEATURES

The activities include grouping suggestions, lists of needed materials, teaching tips, step-by-step directions, and easy Assessment ideas. Some activities also include the following features:

◆ Extensions and Variations—ideas for taking the math skills and concepts further

◆ Home Links—quick and easy activities students can do at home with their families

◆ Writing Connections—suggestions for encouraging students to communicate and reinforce what they've learned through writing.

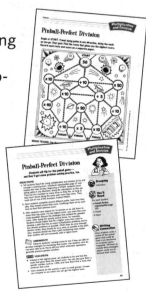

ABOUT GROUPING

Sometimes it's important for students to work together in groups or pairs, to collaborate and communicate. Sometimes they need to work independently. The activities in this book support a variety of needs, from independent to whole class work. You'll find a grouping suggestion at the beginning of each activity.

ASSESSING STUDENTS' WORK

NCTM recommends a variety of approaches to assessment of the various dimensions of a student's mathematical learning. The following assessment suggestions are incorporated throughout this book:

◆ ideas for group and class discussion

◆ ideas for journal writing and written response

◆ ideas for ongoing informal teacher observations

On pages 61–63, you'll also find suggested ways of observing and keeping records of students' work as well as a reproducible student Self-Evaluation Form and an Assessment Checklist and Scoring Rubric.

Remember that you can review students' self-assessments and their journals and written responses to see not only how well they understand concepts but also how well they express their mathematical understandings.

CONNECTIONS TO THE MATH STANDARDS

The activities in this book are designed to support you in meeting the following process standards for students in grades 6–8 recommended by the National Council of Teachers of Mathematics (NCTM):

Problem Solving The activities promote a problem-solving approach to learning. Throughout the book, you'll find suggestions for encouraging students to develop, apply, and explain their problem-solving strategies.

Reasoning & Proof Suggestions in the last step of each activity can serve as prompts to help students draw logical conclusions, explain and justify their thinking, and "pull it together" to make sense of the mathematics skills and concepts they've just used. Activities encourage students to use patterns and relationships as they work.

Communication Activities include ideas for helping students organize and consolidate their mathematical thinking through class discussions and writing connections.

Connections Activities tie to the real world, to the interests of sixth-grade students, and to other areas of the curriculum. The purpose of many activities is to bridge conceptual and procedural knowledge, and to bridge different topics in mathematics.

Representation Students use manipulatives, pictures and diagrams, and numerical representations to complete the activities.

The grids below show how the activities correlate to the other math standards for grades 6–8.

PAGE	Number & Operations	Algebra	Geometry	Measurement	Data Analysis & Probability
8	◆				
9	◆				
11	◆				
12	◆	◆			
14	◆	◆			
16	◆				
17	◆			◆	
18	◆	◆			◆
20	◆				
21	◆				
23					
24			◆		
25			◆		
27		◆	◆		
29		◆	◆	◆	
30	◆		◆		

PAGE	Number & Operations	Algebra	Geometry	Measurement	Data Analysis & Probability
31	◆				
32	◆				
34	◆				
36	◆	◆			
38	◆	◆			
40	◆	◆	◆		
41	◆	◆	◆		
42	◆				◆
43					◆
45					◆
47	◆				◆
49		◆			◆
50	◆				◆
51	◆			◆	
52	◆				
54	◆			◆	

PAGE	Number & Operations	Algebra	Geometry	Measurement	Data Analysis & Probability
55		◆			
57					◆
58		◆			
59	◆	◆	◆		
60	◆	◆	◆		

Source: National Council of Teachers of Mathematics. (2000). *Principles and standards for school mathematics.* Reston: VA: NCTM. www.nctm.org

Any Time Is Math Time

Use these quick activities to keep students' minds on math at the beginning or end of class time, as they are lining up to change classes, or any time you have a few minutes to fill!

1. **Tick-Tock!** Use the classroom clock to give students practice in rounding and estimation.
   - Have them round the current time to the nearest hour or half-hour.
   - Have them see if they can estimate the length of a minute. Ask students to put their heads on their desks so they can't see the clock or their classmates. Have them raise their hands when they think a minute is up.

2. **A Colorful Map** With a map of the United States displayed, have students figure out the least number of colors they would need to color all the states so that no two adjoining states would be the same color.

3. **Chalk It Up** Have students estimate how many pieces of chalk would be needed to color the entire surface area of your classroom chalkboard. Challenge students to figure out a way to check their estimate without using up all your chalk!

4. **How Much Space?** Start a class collection of bottle caps, buttons, or other small items. Have students estimate how much classroom space would be needed to hold 100 of the items. What about 1,000? 5,000?

5. **Let's Lunch** Create math out of lunch statistics.
   - Take a poll of what students bring for lunch on a specific day. Have them create a bar graph with the data.
   - Compare the number of students who bring lunch to the number who buy their lunch in the cafeteria on a given day.
   - Determine if there is a relationship between what students bring for lunch and the person who makes their lunch.

6. **Interior Design** Have students make scale drawings of the classroom. Then ask them to use the drawings to design a way the furniture and other items in the classroom could be arranged. Have students vote on five winning plans. Each month, take a few minutes and rearrange the furniture to suit one of the winning designs.

Grouping

Small groups

You'll Need

◆ Various newspapers or magazines

◆ Pencils

Teaching Tip

Remind students that not all estimates are preceded by words such as *about, more than,* and *nearly.* Tell them that group members must decide what constitutes an estimate. Give assistance if the group requests your help.

Writing Connection

Ask students to be the reporters and write a news article on a local or school event. Have them use exact numbers and estimates in their articles.

Estimation: Read All About It!

All the numbers fit to print are not always exact numbers! Students will see that estimates make the news, too.

DIRECTIONS

1. Divide the class into small groups. Distribute newspapers and magazines and tell each group their goal is to find three articles that have numbers in them. Have students read each of their three articles and highlight or circle each instance in which a number is used.

2. Have the group members classify the numbers in each article as exact numbers or estimates. For example: Hurricane Ethel was 250 miles southeast of Bermuda at 1:35 A.M. Which number is probably exact? Which is probably an estimate? In each case, ask group members to decide why an estimate or an exact number was more appropriate.

3. Ask a member of each group to report the group's findings. Compile the numbers in two lists: exact numbers and estimates. Which were used more often in the news? What generalizations can be made from the lists? For example, are large numbers more often estimates than small numbers are?

ASSESSMENT

Talk with the groups as they work. See if students can generalize examples of numbers found in print that are usually expressed in exact numbers (ages, dates) and numbers that are usually expressed in estimates (crowd sizes, large monetary values like the national debt).

➤➤➤ EXTENSION

Have students look at some numbers that are estimates and decide how a writer might have arrived at each estimate. Did the writer round an exact number up or down, for example, or did he or she make an educated guess?

Invent a Number System!

Students can use their own number system, but can they count in Greek? And can they create a new number system?

DIRECTIONS

1. Ask students if they've ever seen these symbols: I, IV, X, L. They may look like letters, but in ancient Rome they were the symbols for the numbers 1, 4, 10, and 50. Students may have seen them in books or on clockfaces. Tell students they'll learn more about some other number systems.

2. Divide the class into small groups. Hand out reproducible page 10 and have students take a look at the different number systems on it. As a class, compare and contrast the number systems. Ask students to determine which ones are most like our own system and which are least like it.

3. If necessary, point out that the Hindu and Arabic numbers are based on a place-value system with 10 as the base—which is why our system is known as a Hindu-Arabic system! In other bases, symbols were combined to produce a number; the Egyptian 14, for example, would be ||||∩ .What might have inspired the ancient Arabs and Hindus to use 10 as a base? Allow students to share their ideas.

4. Tell each group that they should develop a number system of their own. Encourage them to create a symbol to represent each digit and give each digit—and the number system itself—a name. Ask each group to prepare a presentation to familiarize classmates with the number system they've invented.

ASSESSMENT

Encourage students to include in their presentations a Guess the Number type game or other activity in which the class can evaluate their knowledge of the new number system.

▶▶▶ EXTENSIONS

◆ This activity can be used as part of an interdisciplinary lesson on the development of a culture or nation.

◆ Use this activity if you study different bases, since not all of the civilizations on the reproducible worked in base ten. The Babylonians, for example, used base 60, while the Mayas used base 20.

Grouping
Small groups

You'll Need

For each group:

◆ Invent a Number System! (reproducible page 10)

◆ Pencils

Invent a Number System!

Here are some ways other cultures expressed numerals.
On the back of this page, add your own number system to the list.

EGYPTIAN

1	2	3	4	5	6	7	8	9	10	20	50	100

BABYLONIAN

1	2	3	4	5	6	7	8	9	10	20	50	100

MAYA

.	..	...	....	—	.-.	••	•••	••••	=			
1	2	3	4	5	6	7	8	9	10	20	50	100

HINDU

1	2	3	4	5	6	7	8	9	10	20	50	100

ARABIC

1	2	3	4	5	6	7	8	9	10	20	50	100

GREEK

A	B	Γ	Δ	E	F	Z	H	θ	I	K	N	P
1	2	3	4	5	6	7	8	9	10	20	50	100

ROMAN

I	II	III	IV	V	VI	VII	VIII	IX	X	XX	L	C
1	2	3	4	5	6	7	8	9	10	20	50	100

50+ Super-Fun Math Activities: Grade 6 © 2010 by Scholastic Inc.

Keep 'Em Guessing

Here's a game of mystery—and only decimal place value, guess and check, and logic will help students solve it.

DIRECTIONS

1. Explain to students that they'll work with partners to write and guess mystery numbers. Group students into pairs. Have each student draw six blanks on a sheet of paper, like this: _ _ _ _ _ _.

2. Have each pair decide who will be the keeper of the number and who will be the guesser. Making sure the paper is hidden from the partner, have the keeper fill in his or her blanks with either a 6-digit whole number or a 5-digit decimal number. (In the latter case, the sixth blank should be filled by a decimal point.) Students should not repeat any digits in their numbers.

3. Now have the guesser in each pair try to guess the keeper's number and write the guess on the six blanks. The keeper should check the guess and indicate which digits are correct by:

   ◆ marking a check under a digit or decimal point that is correct and in the right place.

   ◆ marking an X under a digit or decimal point that is correct but in the wrong place.

   ◆ marking an O under a digit or decimal point that is totally wrong (not in the number at all).

   For example, if a guesser wrote 37.904 and the number is actually 394.02, the keeper would mark the guess so it looks like this:

$$\underset{\checkmark}{3}\ \underset{O}{7}\ \underset{X}{.}\ \underset{X}{9}\ \underset{\checkmark}{0}\ \underset{X}{4}$$

4. The guesser should use the information from the keeper to make another guess, to which the keeper should again respond by marking X, O, or check. Play continues until the guesser has guessed the number.

5. Have students reverse roles and play several times to see who can guess a number in the fewest guesses.

ASSESSMENT

On the surface, this is a game about place value, but it also entails problem-solving skills such as guess and check and logic. Encourage students to write down what they learn after each guess so that they will be able to use it in their next guess.

Grouping

Pairs

You'll Need

◆ Paper
◆ Pencils

Writing Connection

Have students write an explanation of the strategies they used when guessing the number.

Pal Around with Palindromes

Students compute the palindromes of whole numbers from 0 to 99—and discover number patterns in the results.

DIRECTIONS

1. Introduce students to the concept of a palindrome: a word or a number that reads the same forward and backward. Ask students to give examples of palindromes and write their suggestions on the chalkboard. Words they may know: *dad, madam, aha.*

2. Show students that almost any number can be turned into a palindrome by reversing the digits and adding the reverse to the original number. Often you must do this several times before arriving at the palindrome. Work this example on the chalkboard.

```
  1,296   (starting number)
+ 6,921   (add the reverse)
  8,217
+ 7,128   (add the reverse)
 15,345
+54,351   (add the reverse)
 69,696   A palindrome!
```

3. Distribute reproducible page 13 and have students find the palindrome of each number. Tell them to use zero as a place holder when figuring palindromes of 1-digit numbers or numbers that end with zero. Ask students to look for patterns as they work.

4. As a class, discuss students' results. Discuss the patterns they find. Some possibilities:
   - The digits in numbers that produce the palindrome 4,884 add up to 15.
   - The palindromes of numbers in which the second digit is twice the first digit are all multiples of 33.
   - The palindromes of multiples of 9 are all 99.

ASSESSMENT
Observe which students discover and use patterns rather than compute every palindrome. For example, by finding the palindrome of 45, they also determine the palindrome of 54.

➡➡➡ EXTENSION
Have students create a time line of events that occurred in palindrome years. This could be a class project.

Grouping
Individual or pairs

You'll Need
For each student or pair:
◆ Pal Around with Palindromes (reproducible page 13)
◆ Pencils

Teaching Tip
Finding the palindrome of 89 and 98 takes 24 steps, making it significantly more difficult to find than others. Have students share their work when computing this palindrome.

Writing Connection
Give students a few examples of word palindromes (*Madam, I'm Adam*) and ask them to create their own.

Pal Around with Palindromes

Circle the numbers that are already palindromes. Then find the palindromes of the remaining numbers from 1 to 99. Write each palindrome in the blank next to the number.

Number	Palindrome	Number	Palindrome	Number	Palindrome	Number	Palindrome	Number	Palindrome
1	____	20	____	40	____	60	____	80	____
2	____	21	____	41	____	61	____	81	____
3	____	22	____	42	____	62	____	82	____
4	____	23	____	43	____	63	____	83	____
5	____	24	____	44	____	64	____	84	____
6	____	25	____	45	____	65	____	85	____
7	____	26	____	46	____	66	____	86	____
8	____	27	____	47	____	67	____	87	____
9	____	28	____	48	____	68	____	88	____
10	____	29	____	49	____	69	____	89	____
11	____	30	____	50	____	70	____	90	____
12	____	31	____	51	____	71	____	91	____
13	____	32	____	52	____	72	____	92	____
14	____	33	____	53	____	73	____	93	____
15	____	34	____	54	____	74	____	94	____
16	____	35	____	55	____	75	____	95	____
17	____	36	____	56	____	76	____	96	____
18	____	37	____	57	____	77	____	97	____
19	____	38	____	58	____	78	____	98	____
		39	____	59	____	79	____	99	____

REMEMBER: To find a palindrome of a number, add the number to its reverse. If the sum isn't a palindrome, add the sum to its reverse. Keep doing that until you get a palindrome.

Pascal's Patterns

Students learn that Pascal's triangle is a three-sided feast of number patterns.

Grouping

Individual

You'll Need

For each student:

◆ Pascal's Patterns (reproducible page 15)

◆ Pencil

DIRECTIONS

1. Distribute reproducible page 15 to students. Explain that the triangle is called Pascal's triangle and that many different number patterns can be found within it. Show students how the triangle works: each number in the triangle is the sum of the two numbers connected to it in the row above.

2. Have students complete the triangle by filling in the blank boxes.

3. Begin to explore the patterns in the triangle. For example:
   ◆ Find the number of times consecutive counting numbers appear.
   ◆ Look for the sequence of triangular numbers.
   ◆ Add the numbers in each row. What number pattern do the sums form? *(Each number is twice the previous number.)*
   ◆ In the diagonal that begins 1, 3, 6..., add the first and second numbers, then the second and third, and so on. What is the pattern? *(consecutive squares)*
   ◆ In the diagonal that begins 1, 4, 10..., add the first two numbers. Then add the third number to that sum, and then the fourth, and so on. What is the pattern in each consecutive sum? Does that pattern happen in any other row? *(The sums are the numbers in the diagonal to the immediate left. Each diagonal running left to right has this property.)*

4. Encourage students to share other patterns they find.

ASSESSMENT

If students have trouble defining certain patterns, make sure they have filled in the boxes in the triangle correctly. **Answers: Row 4:** 1, 4, 6, 4, 1 **Row 5:** 1, 5, 10, 10, 5, 1 **Row 6:** 1, 6, 15, 20, 15, 6, 1 **Row 7:** 1, 7, 21, 35, 35, 21, 7, 1 **Row 8:** 1, 8, 28, 56, 70, 56, 28, 8, 1

▶▶▶ EXTENSION

Have students find out more about the contributions Pascal made to mathematics and the reasons why the triangle bears his name.

Pascal's Patterns

Complete the triangle
by filling in the boxes.

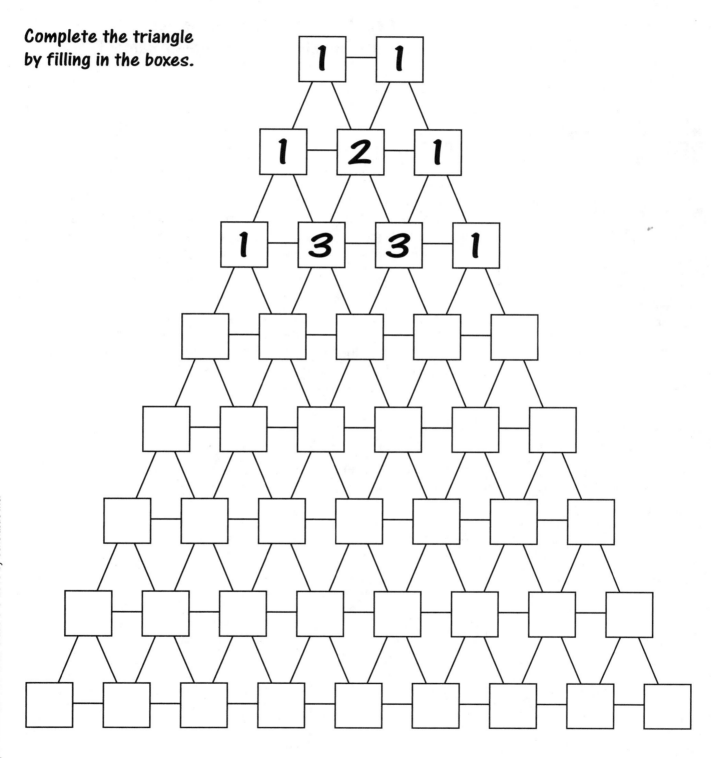

Code Numbers

Students use a letter/number code to give number values to their names.

Grouping

Individual

You'll Need

For each student:

◆ Code Numbers (reproducible page 17)

◆ Pencil

Writing Connection

Ask students to explain whether this statement is true or false, and why: The more letters your name contains, the higher its number value.

PREPARATION

Distribute reproducible page 17 to students. Explain that the code is based on *gematria*, an ancient Hebrew system of number symbolism.

DIRECTIONS

1. Ask students to study the code. Explain that they'll use the code to see whose name is worth the most. You might ask them to speculate first: If their name contains a letter whose number code is in the hundreds, will their total be the highest?

2. Invite students to find the number value of their first name by determining the values of each letter in the name and adding the values. (For example, TRACY would be 200 + 90 + 1 + 3 + 700 = 994.) Have them do the same with their last name, and then add the two values to find the total. When all students have computed their name values, rank the values on the board from least to greatest or greatest to least.

ASSESSMENT

In this type of activity, it is very easy to make a simple computation error. Encourage students to develop a method to check their work when doing the addition.

Code Numbers

A = 1	G = 7	M = 40	S = 100	W = 500
B = 2	H = 8	N = 50	T = 200	X = 600
C = 3	I = 9	O = 60	U = 300	Y = 700
D = 4	J = 10	P = 70	V = 400	Z = 800
E = 5	K = 20	Q = 80		
F = 6	L = 30	R = 90		

NUMBER VALUE

My First Name:

_____   _____

My Last Name:

_____   _____

TOTAL: _____

Grouping

Whole class

You'll Need

For each student:

◆ **Chain of Fools (reproducible page 19)**

◆ Counters

◆ Pencils

◆ Calculator (optional)

Chain of Fools

Geometric progressions show your students that collecting on a chain letter is mathematically impossible!

DIRECTIONS

1. Tell students that although chain letters involving money are illegal in the United States, some people still send them. Ask any students who have ever received a chain letter to explain how the letter worked.

2. Then ask students to imagine they've received a chain letter containing a list of ten names. They're told to send $1 to the person at the top of the list, add their own name to the bottom of the list, and send a copy of the letter to five friends. As the chain keeps going, the sender's name travels farther up the list. When it reaches the top, the chain letter promises, the sender will receive thousands of dollars! But could making money be this easy? Challenge students to find out.

3. Act out the first two "mailings" with the class. Give one student the role of letter writer. In the first round of the chain letter, that student chooses five classmates to be recipients of the chain letter. In the next round, each of those five classmates picks five different classmates to represent the next round of recipients. Ask students if they think there are enough students remaining to complete a third mailing.

4. Suggest that students use counters or draw a diagram to model round 3 and round 4. Then distribute reproducible page 19 and have students complete it.

ASSESSMENT

Students should see that the number of recipients in each round can be found by multiplying 5 (the number of people each letter writer sends a letter to) by itself the same number of times as that round. **Answers: Round 1: 5 Round 2: 25 Round 3: 125 Round 4: 625 Round 5: 3,125 Round 6: 15,625 Round 7: 78,125 Round 8: 390,625 Round 9: 1,953,125 Round 10: 9,765,625 Total: 12,207,031 (adding the first letter writer)**

Chain of Fools

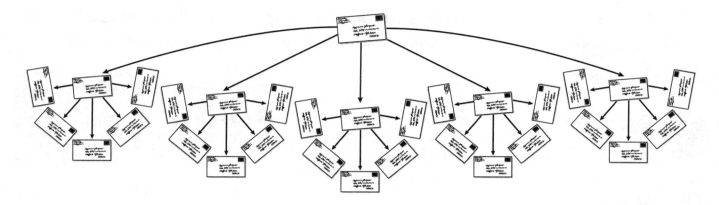

MAILING ROUND	NUMBER OF PEOPLE WHO RECEIVE LETTER IN THIS ROUND

ROUND 1 . . . . 5 _____

ROUND 2 . . . . $5 \times 5 =$ _____

ROUND 3 . . . . $5 \times 5 \times 5 =$ _____

ROUND 4 . . . . $5 \times 5 \times 5 \times 5 =$ _____

ROUND 5 . . . . $5 \times 5 \times 5 \times 5 \times 5 =$ _____

ROUND 6 . . . . $5 \times 5 \times 5 \times 5 \times 5 \times 5 =$ _____

ROUND 7 . . . . $5 \times 5 \times 5 \times 5 \times 5 \times 5 \times 5 =$ _____

ROUND 8 . . . . $5 \times 5 \times 5 \times 5 \times 5 \times 5 \times 5 \times 5 =$ _____

ROUND 9 . . . . . . $5 \times 5 \times 5 \times 5 \times 5 \times 5 \times 5 \times 5 \times 5 =$ _____

ROUND 10 . . . $5 \times 5 \times 5 \times 5 \times 5 \times 5 \times 5 \times 5 \times 5 \times 5 =$ _____

TOTAL NUMBER OF PEOPLE WHO RECEIVE LETTER: _____

Chocolate-Covered Factors

Students will discover why some kinds of chocolate bars come in 12 pieces, as they use division to share.

Grouping

Small groups

You'll Need

◆ Chocolate bars divided into 12 equal sections, one bar per group

Teaching Tip

In place of real chocolate bars, you can make a copy of the model for each group.

Writing Connection

Have students make a list of other types of foods that are sold in easily divisible numbers.

DIRECTIONS

1. Give a chocolate bar or model to each group. Ask students how the bar could be shared evenly by two people. Then ask each group to prepare a chart showing all the other ways the bar could be evenly divided. In each instance, the chart should include the number of people sharing the bar and the number of whole pieces each person would get.

CHOC-O-LOTS!	CHOC-O-LOTS!	CHOC-O-LOTS!	CHOC-O-LOTS!
CHOC-O-LOTS!	CHOC-O-LOTS!	CHOC-O-LOTS!	CHOC-O-LOTS!
CHOC-O-LOTS!	CHOC-O-LOTS!	CHOC-O-LOTS!	CHOC-O-LOTS!

2. Have students repeat with an 8-section, 10-section, 14-section, and 20-section bar.

3. When groups have completed their charts, talk with students about the results. Which bars were able to be divided in the most ways? Students should realize that the more factors a number has, the more ways it can be divided. For example, since 12 has more factors (1, 2, 3, 4, 6, and 12) than 10 (1, 2, 5, and 10), a chocolate bar divided into 12 pieces can be shared in more ways than a bar divided into 10 pieces.

ASSESSMENT

Observe students' charts to see that they've found all the factors of each number. Suggest that they use manipulatives if they're having difficulty with the "chocolate bars" of 8, 10, 14, and 20 pieces.

✛✛✛ VARIATION

This activity can also be used as a lesson on equivalent fractions. By dividing a 12-piece chocolate bar in half, for example, students can see that $\frac{1}{2}$ is equal to $\frac{6}{12}$, since there are 6 chocolate pieces in $\frac{1}{2}$ of the bar.

Number of people who share	Number of pieces each person gets
2	6

Pinball-Perfect Division

Students will flip for this pinball game— and they'll get some problem-solving practice, too.

DIRECTIONS

1. Tell students they'll be using multiplication and division to try and compile a winning score. Distribute reproducible page 22 and explain the rules of play. Beginning at START, students travel along paths in any direction, doing the calculations as they go. They can hit a bumper as many times as they like, as long as they don't travel along the same path more than once. They must exit at one of the bumpers marked FINISH.

2. Have students complete several different paths. Each time they play, they should record their score. Challenge them to try each time to beat their previous score.

3. After students have played for 10 minutes or so, ask them to share their top score. For the highest score, was more than one route possible? Discuss the strategies that yielded the greatest score. After doing the activity several times, for example, students should realize that for a higher score they need to develop a path that has as many multiplication problems and as few division problems as possible. When they do cross through division circles, they should do so as early as possible in the path. Also, students should see that a path containing more circles than another will not necessarily yield a higher score.

ASSESSMENT

Observe students' running scores to see if they are able to develop strategies for increasing their scores. Ask students who do not seem able to do this to tell you which arithmetic operations generally produce greater numbers.

✛✛✛ VARIATIONS

◆ Instead of the highest score, ask students to try and find the route that gives them the lowest score. You can also give them a specific number, such as 1,000, and have them find a route that produces that score.

◆ Have students do this activity in pairs or small groups. Groups can compete to see which one can get the highest score.

Grouping

Individual

You'll Need

For each student:

◆ **Pinball Perfect Division (reproducible page 22)**

◆ Pencil

◆ Paper

Writing Connection

Have students write a review of the pinball game that could be used in an electronics or computer game magazine. Tell them to include three strategies players could use to increase their scores.

Pinball-Perfect Division

Begin at START. Travel along paths in any direction, doing the math as you go. Your goal: Find the route that gives you the highest score. Record each route and score on a separate paper.

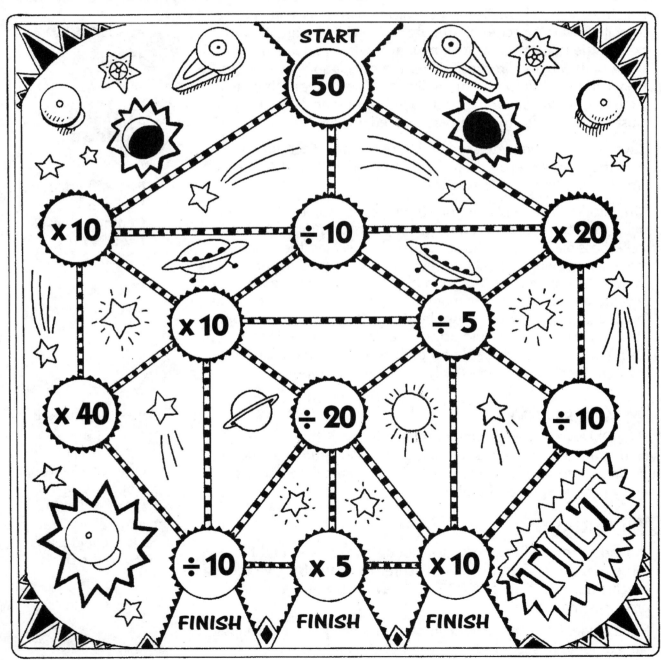

BRAIN TEASER: For the highest score, is more than one route possible? _____

How Many M&Ms?

Students examine different methods of estimation to see which is most efficient and most accurate.

PREPARATION

Before class, write the three estimation options, given in step 2 below, on the chalkboard or on an overhead projector. Make sure students cannot see them until you describe them in step 2. It will save time if you count the number of candies in the bag before class.

DIRECTIONS

1. Pour the bag of candy into the jar. Ask students if they can guess, just by looking, how many candies the jar contains. Have students explain their guesses as they offer them.

2. Display your list of estimation methods:
   - Find the amount in one ounce of candy and multiply by the number of ounces in the bag
   - Find the number of candies of one color and multiply by the number of colors in the bag
   - Find the number of quarter cups in the bag; then find the number of candies in one quarter cup and multiply by the number of quarter cups in the bag

   Give students a few minutes to explain any additional estimation methods they would like to try.

3. Have groups test each estimation method listed. In each case, record both the estimate and the time it took to get the estimate.

4. Tell students the actual number of candies in the jar. Compare that number to the estimates they found. As a class, decide which estimation method worked best, keeping in mind the amount of time each took as well as the accuracy of the estimate.

ASSESSMENT

Note how students evaluate the various estimation methods. They should understand that some methods are more accurate than others, even though they are more difficult to perform.

Grouping

Whole class

You'll Need

- Large bag of M&Ms or other multicolor candies
- Glass jar or other clear container that can hold the candy
- Standard measurement scale
- Quarter-cup measuring cup
- Clock or watch with a minute hand

Teaching Tip

You can do this activity with small groups of students. Each group can test a different estimation method.

You'll Need

For each student:
- 2 strips of paper, 2 inches by 12 inches
- Tape
- Scissors
- Crayons or markers

One-Sided Wonder

Students explore topology by making a Möbius strip and comparing it to a close variation.

PREPARATION

Cut the paper strips out of plain white or construction paper. (Do not use heavy paper or cardboard.)

DIRECTIONS

1. Distribute one paper strip to each student. Point out that the paper strip has two sides. Then ask students to figure out how they could change the paper so it has only one side. Allow them to brainstorm for a few minutes.

2. Show students how to twist the strip once (as in Figure A) and then bring the ends together and tape them in place (Figure B).

Figure A   Figure B   Figure C

3. Tell students to color the inside of the circle one color and the outside another color. Discuss what happens. Explain that they've created a shape called a Möbius strip.

4. Have students cut the strip down the middle (Figure C). What happens now?

5. Give each student another paper strip. Have them repeat step 2 with the second strip, twist it twice before taping. Then have them try steps 3 and 4. What happens?

ASSESSMENT

Students should see that the strip with one twist has only one side. When the strip is twisted twice, however, it retains its two-sided qualities. See if students can use this fact to predict what will happen when different numbers of twists are added to the strip.

✦✦✦ VARIATION

Give students two paper strips. Have them color each side of the strips a different color. Then have them make circles as before, twisting one of the strips once and one twice. Have them look at the taped ends of each strip. What do they notice about the colors? How can that help them predict when a circle is a Möbius strip?

What a Square!

Students create their own tangrams to discover properties of shapes.

DIRECTIONS

1. Tell students that they are going to make a collection of tangram pieces. When they're finished folding and cutting they'll have five triangles, a small square, and a parallelogram. The challenge—to fit them back together to form a large square.

2. Distribute reproducible page 26, a sheet of paper, and scissors to each student. Students can follow the directions on the reproducible to make their tangrams, or you can have them follow along with you to fold and cut their papers.

3. When students have their seven tangram pieces cut, ask them to make a square using two tangram pieces, then three, and then all seven.

4. Discuss some of the interesting properties of tangrams students discover.

ASSESSMENT

Students should be able to recognize each of the figures that make up the tangram puzzle, along with the trapezoid that's produced in step 4 of the activity.

➡➡➡ EXTENSION

Ask students to see how many different designs or objects they can create using all or some of the tangram pieces.

Grouping

Individual

You'll Need

For each student:

◆ **What a Square! (reproducible page 26)**

◆ Paper, 8½ by 11 inches

◆ Scissors

What a Square!

Start with a piece of paper 8½ inches by 11 inches.
Follow these directions to make tangram pieces.

1. Fold one corner of the paper over, cut along the top and discard the extra piece.

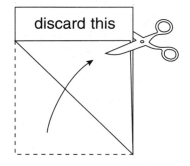

2. Make two large triangles by folding the square diagonally and cutting along the fold.

3. Take one of the large triangles. Make two smaller triangles by folding it in half and cutting along the fold.

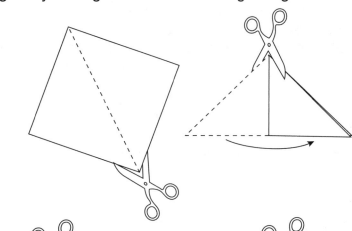

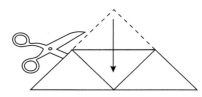

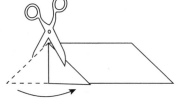

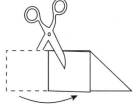

4. Take the other large triangle. Mark the midpoint of the base. Fold the top of the triangle down to meet the midpoint. Cut along the fold to make a smaller triangle and a trapezoid.

5. Fold one corner of the trapezoid to the midpoint and cut along the fold, making a small triangle.

6. Use the remainder of the trapezoid. Fold the non-pointed end into the midpoint and cut along the fold, creating a small square.

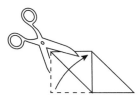

7. Use the remaining piece. To create a triangle and parallelogram, fold the bottom left corner up to the top right corner and cut along the fold.

▶▶▶ **Now make shapes with your tangram pieces.**
Can you put the large square back together again?

50+ Super-Fun Math Activities: Grade 6 © 2010 by Scholastic Inc.

Without a Trace

Students do some "networking" by using vertices and line segments to determine the solvability of network puzzles.

DIRECTIONS

1. Introduce network puzzles by drawing the trial figures on the chalkboard. Ask volunteers to trace each figure without lifting the chalk. What do students discover? Do students think they could predict whether a network puzzle can be traced?

2. Distribute reproducible page 28. Ask students to predict if each figure can be traced. Then give them time to try each one.

3. If students have not discovered which puzzles can be solved after 15 to 20 minutes, show them that figures A and E can be traced by starting at one point and ending up at a different point, while figures B and D can be traced by starting at one point and ending at the same point. Figures C and F cannot be traced.

4. Have students complete the chart at the bottom of the reproducible by counting the number of "odd" and "even" vertices each figure contains. ("Odd" vertices have an odd number of line segments; "even" vertices have an even number of line segments. Figure A, for example, contains two odd vertices and four even vertices.) Make sure that students understand that a vertex is any meeting of two or more line segments. In the example, for instance, the vertex B is an odd vertex, formed by three line segments: *AB, BC,* and *DB.*

5. When students have finished, ask them to draw some conclusions about predicting whether a network puzzle can be solved. Help students make these generalizations:

   ◆ Networks containing only even vertices can be traced by starting at any point and ending up back at that point.

   ◆ Networks containing exactly two odd vertices can be traced by starting at one of the odd vertices and ending up at the other.

   ◆ Networks containing any other number of odd vertices cannot be traced.

➔➔➔ EXTENSION

Have students draw some network puzzles of their own and exchange them with classmates.

Grouping
Individual

You'll Need
For each student:
◆ **Without a Trace (reproducible page 28)**
◆ Pencil

TRIAL FIGURES

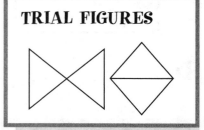

VERTEX EXAMPLE

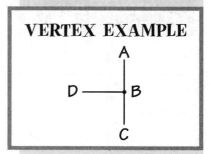

Name _____

Without a Trace

Try to trace each design without lifting your pencil from the paper or going back over a line you've already traced. Check the ones that can be traced.

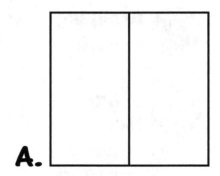

A.

B.

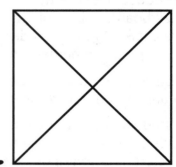

C.

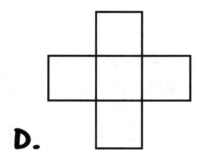

D.

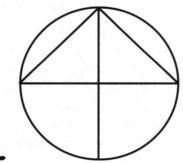

E.

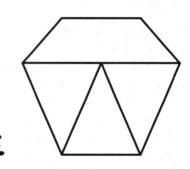

F.

FIGURE	NUMBER OF ODD VERTICES	NUMBER OF EVEN VERTICES	CAN IT BE TRACED?
A			
B			
C			
D			
E			
F			

Table Manners

It's party time! Students will relate area and perimeter by figuring out how many people they can seat at one table.

DIRECTIONS

1. Ask students to imagine they have six square tables that they want to push together to create one large table. Each of the square tables seats only one person on each side. They want to fit as many people as possible at the big table. How should they arrange the six tables to fit the most people? Show students that each small table must touch at least one side of another small table, as shown.

2. Distribute the square counters and have students determine several solutions to the problem. After students have worked independently for a few minutes, ask volunteers to draw their ideas on the chalkboard.

3. Once they've determined the greatest number of people that can be seated at the big table (14), have students determine the fewest number that can be seated (10). Discuss their results. Students might think that because the area of the big table will always be six square units, the big table will always seat the same number of people, whatever the arrangement. With several solutions on the chalkboard, students should realize that the number of people seated has to do with the perimeter of the big table, not the area.

ASSESSMENT

Ask students to describe their strategies for solving the problem. They should be able to articulate that the goal is to create a shape with the largest possible perimeter.

VARIATION

Students might use their desks or six small tables to model the problem.

Grouping

Individual

You'll Need

For each student:
◆ 6 square counters

Teaching Tip

You can substitute six small construction paper squares for the counters.

Writing Connection

Ask students to try the same activity with 8 "tables" and then write a rule or generalization for finding the maximum seating. Tell students they can draw some illustrations to help explain their rule.

Grouping

Small groups

You'll Need

For each group:

◆ Centimeter tape measure

◆ Paper

◆ Pencils

Teaching Tip

If it's too difficult for students to do this activity as a scavenger hunt, have them gather a variety of circular objects and do the activity as a class.

Writing Connection

Ask students to explain how they could use the formula $C = \pi d$ to find either the circumference or diameter of a circle if they know the other.

Scavenging Circles

This scavenger hunt will have students running around in circles—and learning about pi.

PREPARATION

Prepare a list of circular items that students are to find on their scavenger hunt. Try to choose objects of different sizes, such as coins, coasters, jar lids, rolls of tape, Frisbees, bicycle tires, plates, and cooking pot lids.

DIRECTIONS

1. Divide the class into groups of four or five. Give each group the list of circular items and ask them to gather as many of the items as they can find. You can devote class time to the hunt, or have students divide the list among the group members and search for the items at home.

2. After students have gathered their items, have students measure the circumference and diameter of each one and record the results. Suggest that students make a chart such as this:

Object	Circumference	Diameter	Circumference Divided by Diameter

3. Ask students to study the measurements to see if they can find a relationship between the circumference and diameter of each circular object. If they express the ratio of circumference to diameter for each circle, what similarities do they see? Suggest that students try dividing each object's circumference by its diameter. They should see that the circumference is always about three times the diameter.

4. You may want to explain that a formula expresses the relationship between the circumference and diameter of any circle, where the circumference *(C)* is equal to about 3.14 times the diameter *(d)*. The value of 3.14 is called pi (π) and the formula is expressed $C = \pi d$.

ASSESSMENT

Observe students' accuracy in measuring the circumference and diameter of each circular object. They will be more successful finding a relationship if they measure accurately.

Fraction Magic

Using a magic square, students discover that properties of addition apply to fractions as well as whole numbers.

DIRECTIONS

1. Display the magic square shown on the chalkboard or overhead projector. Review the concept of a magic square: It's a grid of numbers in which each row, column, and diagonal add up to the same sum. Ask students to confirm this with the magic square on the chalkboard.

4	3	8
9	5	1
2	7	6

2. Ask students what they think might happen if the same number were added to each of the numbers in the magic square. Would the square still work? After a short discussion, have students pick a number and try it.

3. Ask students if they think the magic square would work if it contained fractions rather than whole numbers. Then have them change the whole numbers in the original square to fractions. One possibility: Use the whole numbers as numerators and select one number as a common denominator. By selecting 10 as a denominator, for example, the revised magic square would look like this:

$\frac{2}{5}$	$\frac{3}{10}$	$\frac{4}{5}$
$\frac{9}{10}$	$\frac{1}{2}$	$\frac{1}{10}$
$\frac{1}{5}$	$\frac{7}{10}$	$\frac{3}{5}$

4. Have students test their squares by adding up the rows, columns, and diagonals.

5. Finally, pose this question: Would the new square work if the same fraction were added to each of the fractions in the square? Have students pick a fraction to add, test the theory, and discuss the results.

▶▶▶ EXTENSION
Have students try turning the whole numbers in the original square into fractions by using the original numbers as denominators rather than numerators. Does the square work? Why or why not?

Grouping
Individual

You'll Need
◆ Paper
◆ Pencils

Subtractin' Fractions

Are students having trouble subtracting fractions? This game should make things perfectly clear.

Grouping

Individual

You'll Need

For each student:

◆ **Subtractin' Fractions (reproducible page 33)**

◆ Scissors

◆ Paper clip

◆ Pencil

Writing Connection

Ask students to determine the fewest and most number of spins they'd need to clear the 1 strip and explain their reasoning in a few sentences.

DIRECTIONS

1. Explain to students that they'll be playing a fraction game. The goal is to clear a fraction strip by removing fractions from a whole. Distribute reproducible page 33. Demonstrate how to use the spinner, by spinning a paper clip around the point of a pencil placed at the center of the spinner. Have students cut out the spinner and each of the fraction strips. Then have them cut the ½, ¼, ⅛, and 1/16 strips along the dotted lines.

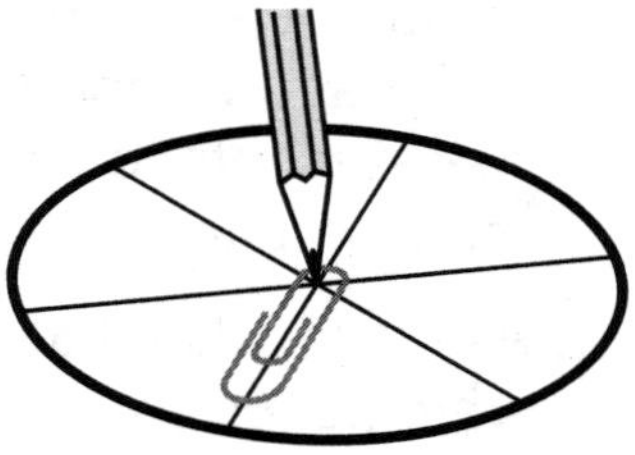

2. Ask students to place the strip representing 1 whole on their desk and place the two ½ pieces on top of it. Have each student spin his or her spinner. The student must remove the fraction spun from the 1 strip. To do this, the student may need to replace a ½ piece with others that add up to an equivalent value. For example, a student who spins ⅛ can replace one of the ½ pieces with four ⅛ pieces and then remove one ⅛ piece.

3. Have students continue spinning and removing fractions until their 1 strips are clear. (They must clear the 1 strips in an exact spin.)

ASSESSMENT

Observe students' understanding of equivalent fractions as they subtract. They will probably realize, for example, that four ⅛ pieces equal one ½ piece, but they may not immediately grasp that they can reach ½ by combining two ⅛s and one ¼ or four 1/16s and two ⅛s.

VARIATION

Played backward, this activity can give students practice in fraction addition. Have them start with an empty 1 strip and, as they spin, add fractions to the strip until they've put the two ½ pieces in position.

Subtractin' Fractions

Use these fraction pieces to play the game.

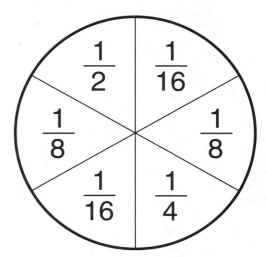

1

$\dfrac{1}{2}$	$\dfrac{1}{2}$

$\dfrac{1}{4}$	$\dfrac{1}{4}$	$\dfrac{1}{4}$	$\dfrac{1}{4}$

$\dfrac{1}{8}$	$\dfrac{1}{8}$	$\dfrac{1}{8}$	$\dfrac{1}{8}$	$\dfrac{1}{8}$	$\dfrac{1}{8}$	$\dfrac{1}{8}$	$\dfrac{1}{8}$

$\dfrac{1}{16}$	$\dfrac{1}{16}$	$\dfrac{1}{16}$	$\dfrac{1}{16}$	$\dfrac{1}{16}$	$\dfrac{1}{16}$	$\dfrac{1}{16}$	$\dfrac{1}{16}$	$\dfrac{1}{16}$	$\dfrac{1}{16}$	$\dfrac{1}{16}$	$\dfrac{1}{16}$	$\dfrac{1}{16}$	$\dfrac{1}{16}$	$\dfrac{1}{16}$	$\dfrac{1}{16}$

Decimal Medalists

Let the Games begin! Students use decimal place value to learn about Olympic medalists of the past.

DIRECTIONS

1. Explain to students that they're going to find out some interesting information about medal winners of past Olympics. To do this, they'll have to compare decimals. If necessary, review decimal comparisons. You may want to draw a place value chart on the board or an overhead projector. Remind students that they must compare both whole numbers and decimals to determine which number is smallest and which is largest.

hundreds	tens	ones	.	tenths	hundredths	thousandths
6	5	4	.	3	2	1

2. Distribute reproducible page 35 and have students complete it. Encourage them to use the place value chart if they need help. Make sure students remember that they should order from smallest number to largest when looking at times, and largest to smallest when looking at points or distances.

ASSESSMENT

Students should understand that one number isn't larger than another simply because it contains more places (for example, .673 versus .9). **Answers: 1924:** bronze, silver, gold **1964:** bronze, gold, silver **1976:** gold, bronze, silver **1980:** bronze, silver, gold **1992:** bronze, silver, gold **1996:** bronze, gold, silver

Decimal Medalists

Order the numbers in each group to discover who won the gold, silver, and bronze medal. Write the correct medal in the blank next to the athlete's name.

REMEMBER:

* If the decimals are times, the smallest number gets the gold.
* If the decimals are distances or points, the largest number gets the gold.

1924—PARIS, FRANCE
Track and field: men's long jump

_____ Sverre Hansen, Norway
(7.26 meters)

_____ Edward Gourdin, United States
(7.275 meters)

_____ William DeHart Hubbard,
United States (7.445 meters)

1964—TOKYO, JAPAN
Men's gymnastics: still rings

_____ Boris Shacklin, Soviet Union
(19.4 points)

_____ Takuji Hayata, Japan
(19.475 points)

_____ Franco Menichelli, Italy
(19.425 points)

1976—MONTREAL, CANADA
Women's swimming: 100-meter butterfly

_____ Kornelia Ender, East Germany
(1 minute, 0.13 second)

_____ Wendy Boglioli, United States
(1 minute, 1.17 seconds)

_____ Andrea Pollack, East Germany
(1 minute, 0.98 second)

1980—MOSCOW, SOVIET UNION
Men's swimming: 400-meter freestyle

_____ Ivar Stukolkin, Soviet Union
(3 minutes, 53.95 seconds)

_____ Andrei Krylov, Soviet Union
(3 minutes, 53.24 seconds)

_____ Vladimir Salnikov, Soviet Union
(3 minutes, 51.31 seconds)

1992—BARCELONA, SPAIN
**Women's gymnastics:
individual all-around**

_____ Lavinia Milosovici, Romania
(39.687 points)

_____ Shannon Miller, United States
(39.725 points)

_____ Tatiana Goutsou, Ukraine
(39.737 points)

1996—ATLANTA, GEORGIA
Track and field: women's 800-meter run

_____ Maria Mutola Lurdes, Mozambique
(1 minute, 58.71 seconds)

_____ Svetlana Masterkova, Russia
(1 minute, 57.73 seconds)

_____ Ana Quirot Fidelia, Cuba
(1 minute, 58.11 seconds)

Mamma Mia, Whatta Pizza!

Can students finish off a whole pizza?
They can if they know how to compute with decimals!

DIRECTIONS

1. Tell students they'll be using operations with decimals to polish off a pizza. If necessary, review how to add, subtract, multiply, and divide with decimals. Remind students that when they add and subtract, they should be careful to align the decimal points. When they multiply or divide, they must count decimal places and be sure the decimal point is correctly placed in the product or quotient.

2. Distribute reproducible page 37. Explain to students that they can pick any number greater than 0 to start. They should write that number in the START space on the pizza. By following the operations signs on each piece of pepperoni, they should return to their own start number each time they get to a mushroom!

3. When everyone has completed the pizza, talk with students about their results. See if students can figure out why the puzzle works. They should realize that it has to do with inverse operations—if something is done to a number, then it must be "undone" at some point in the series.

ASSESSMENT

If students aren't getting back to the start number, most likely they are making mathematical errors. Encourage them to use calculators, particularly in the later series of the puzzle, or to work together to solve portions of the puzzle.

✛✛✛ VARIATIONS

◆ You may want to approach the activity in stages. Ask students to first pick a whole number and see if the puzzle works. Then have them choose a decimal number and try it.

◆ Students working with integers can predict whether the puzzle will work if a negative number is used and then test their hypothesis.

Grouping

Individual

You'll Need

For each student:

◆ Mamma Mia, Whatta Pizza! (reproducible page 37)

◆ Pencil

◆ Calculator (optional)

Mamma Mia, Whatta Pizza!

Pick a number greater than 0, and write it in the START pepperoni.
Then follow the arrows, doing the math as you go. You should arrive
back at your own START number at each mushroom. Yum!

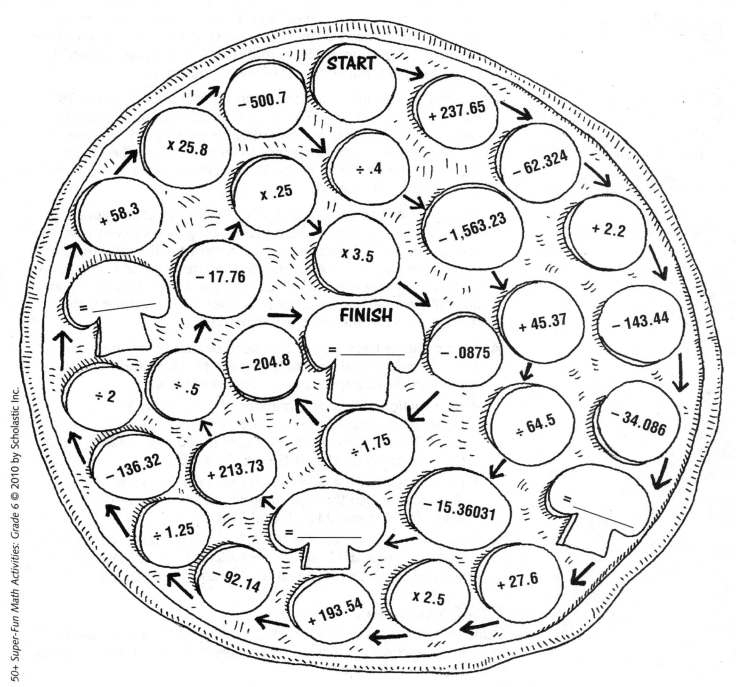

Grouping

Pairs

You'll Need

For each pair:

◆ **Could You Repeat That? (reproducible page 39)**

◆ Scissors

Could You Repeat That?

Get students concentrating on equivalent fractions and repeating decimals—and the patterns found in them!

DIRECTIONS

1. Ask students to convert these two fractions to decimals: ²⁄₇, ²⁄₅. If necessary, remind them they need to divide the numerator by the denominator to do this. What do students discover about the decimals? Explain to students that they'll play a game in which they will match fractions and repeating decimals.

2. Divide the class into pairs and hand out reproducible page 39. Have them cut out the 36 fraction/repeating decimal squares and place them facedown on a desk. Have students mix the squares so that neither partner can identify them. Then have students arrange the squares—still facedown—so they re-form a six-by-six game board.

3. The object of the game is to find equivalent fraction/repeating decimal pairs. Students take turns selecting two squares from the board. If a student uncovers an equivalent fraction and repeating decimal, he or she removes the two squares from the board and takes another turn. If not, his or her turn is over. Play continues until all the matches have been uncovered. The winner is the student who has the most matching pairs.

4. After students have played the game several times, ask them if they noticed any patterns between the fractions and their equivalent repeating decimals. Here are some ideas:

   ◆ Any fraction with a denominator of 7 can be written as a repeating decimal containing the same six digits in the same order. The fraction ¹⁄₇, for example, is equal to $.\overline{142857}$, and the fraction ⁵⁄₇ can be written as $.\overline{714285}$.

   ◆ Any fraction with a denominator of 9 can be written as a decimal in which the repeating digit is the numerator. For example, ²⁄₉ is equal to $.\overline{2}$, and ⁷⁄₉ is equal to $.\overline{7}$.

   ◆ Fractions with denominators of 11 form repeating decimals in which the repeating digits are multiples of 9. For example, ¹⁄₁₁ is equal to $.\overline{09}$, ²⁄₁₁ is equal to $.\overline{18}$, and ³⁄₁₁ is equal to $.\overline{27}$.

✚✚✚ VARIATION

Students can make Concentration game boards to practice other mathematical concepts. For example, they can pair names of figures with pictures of the figures.

Could You Repeat That?

Cut out these squares.
Match fractions and decimal equivalents.

$\frac{1}{3}$	$\frac{2}{3}$	$\frac{1}{7}$	$\frac{3}{7}$	$\frac{2}{9}$	$\frac{5}{9}$
$\frac{6}{11}$	$\frac{10}{11}$	$\frac{5}{6}$	$\frac{5}{12}$	$\frac{7}{15}$	$\frac{1}{6}$
$\frac{15}{22}$	$\frac{1}{22}$	$\frac{1}{18}$	$\frac{11}{15}$	$\frac{3}{11}$	$\frac{11}{12}$
$.\overline{3}$	$.\overline{6}$	$.\overline{142857}$	$.\overline{428571}$	$.\overline{2}$	$.\overline{5}$
$.\overline{54}$	$.\overline{90}$	$.8\overline{3}$	$.41\overline{6}$	$.4\overline{6}$	$.1\overline{6}$
$.6\overline{81}$	$.0\overline{45}$	$.05$	$.7\overline{3}$	$.\overline{27}$	$.91\overline{6}$

50+ Super-Fun Math Activities: Grade 6 © 2010 by Scholastic Inc.

Name _____

Problems and More

Put on your thinking cap to solve these problems.

1. CALCU-CHANGE

Display the number 2,753 on your calculator. List three ways you could change the 7 to an 8 without clearing the display. (Hint: Other numbers could also change.)

2. FACING UP

These are all different views of the same cube. What design belongs on the missing face of the fourth cube?

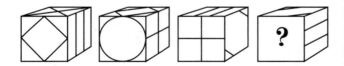

3. X MARKS THE SPOT

Place five Xs in the grid below so that there's no more than one X in each row, column, or diagonal. Can you do it more than one way?

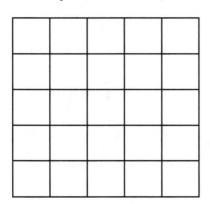

4. YOU'VE GOT THE ANSWERS

You've got the answers to the equations in this grid. Use the numbers 2, 3, 4, 5, 6, 12, 14, and 28 to fill in the empty boxes to make all six equations true. (Hint: You'll have to use one of the numbers twice.)

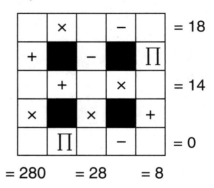

5. BOXED IN

Pick one number from each column below. Make sure none of the numbers you pick are in the same row. Add the five numbers you picked. Then repeat the previous steps several times. What do you notice about the sums you get?

1	2	3	4	5
6	7	8	9	10
11	12	13	14	15
16	17	18	19	20
21	22	23	24	25

50+ Super-Fun Math Activities: Grade 6 © 2010 by Scholastic Inc.

Answers on page 64.

Problems and More

6. GAME, SET, MATCH!

There are 28 players in the Math Town women's singles tennis tournament. It's a single elimination tournament—pairs play each other, and the winner of each match moves on to the next round. How many matches must be played?

_____

7. ROUND-UP TIME!

A count of the cowboys and cattle at the XY Squared ranch produces the following information: There are a total of 17 heads and 56 legs. How many cowboys and how many cows are on the ranch?

_____

8. WATCH OUT

The top cog in this watch turns to the right. In which direction does the bottom cog turn?

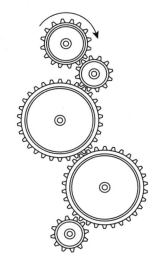

9. LUCK O' THE IRISH

What luck—a whole field full of four-leaf clovers! Can you spit the field into four identical pieces that each contain the same number of clovers?

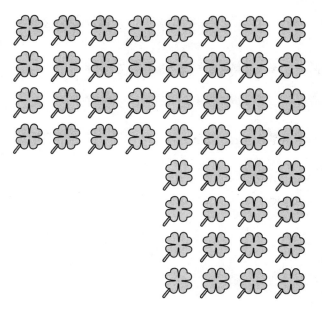

10. MAKING THE GRADE

Pete has gotten math grades of 78, 91, and 94. He wants a 90 average by report card time. What grade will he need on his last math test to accomplish this?

_____

Nutritious Averages

With some raisins or cereal in hand, students can learn more about averages.

Grouping

Small groups (even numbers)

You'll Need

◆ Several boxes of raisins or shaped cereal

◆ Small paper cups or muffin papers

Teaching Tip

You can count out even numbers of raisins or pieces of cereal to make sure amounts will be evenly distributed and avoid arguments!

Writing Connection

Ask students to make a list of real instances, in school and outside of school, where averages are used.

PREPARATION

You may want to divide up the cereal or raisins before class. Place small amounts in paper cups, allowing for one cup per student. Make sure the cups hold different amounts.

DIRECTIONS

1. Distribute the cups of raisins. Tell each student to guess the number of raisins in his or her cup. Record their guesses. Then have students count, and have the groups record the number of raisins each member starts with. Ask one member of each group to add and divide to find, mathematically, the average number of raisins (rounded to the nearest 1) the group has.

2. Tell students they'll do a series of trades to see how averaging really works. Divide the class into groups of even numbers and ask the members of each group to pair up. Then have pairs divide their raisins so both partners have about the same number. If one group member has 4 raisins and the other has 9, for example, they divide them so that one person has 6 and the other has 7 (the group member who has more to start with keeps the extra.) Have the groups record the new number of raisins each member has.

3. Have the groups do several more rounds of swapping and recording. (Make sure group members find a different partner within their group for each round.) Then talk about the activity. Ask students to compare their individual numbers to the group's original average. Students should notice that as more exchanges are done, more and more group members will have the same number of raisins, and that the number is the same as (or close to) the average number of raisins computed at the beginning of the activity.

✦✦✦ VARIATION

Give each group a larger number of raisins to start with. Ask them to figure out a way they could determine the average number of raisins for each group member without computing the average.

Forecast Lineup

Students put together a double-line graph to determine which local weather forecast is really the most reliable.

PREPARATION
Make a list of the local television stations in your area that produce their own weather forecasts.

DIRECTIONS
1. Divide the class into groups—one group for each local television weather forecast. Tell students they are going to conduct a test to see which station produces the most accurate weather forecast. Pick a starting day, and have students watch the five-day forecast of their assigned TV station. They'll need to write down the forecast high temperature for each day.

2. As a class, keep track of the actual high temperatures over the same five days. Get as accurate a reading as possible—ideally, you should use the temperatures taken at a local airport or reported by the National Weather Service.

3. Distribute reproducible page 44 to each group. Have students plot the five-day forecast highs on the graph. Have them connect each set of data with a solid line. Have students plot their data for actual five-day temperatures on their graphs as well, using a dashed line.

4. Display the completed graphs. Have students compare the data for each station and decide which station had the most accurate weather forecast. Students should understand that for each set of data—forecast high temperature and actual high temperature—the closer the lines are, the more accurate the forecast.

ASSESSMENT
Observe that students have recorded their data accurately. Then ask questions about the graph to see if individual students can interpret the data.

➤➤➤ EXTENSION
Invite a meteorologist from the winning TV station or elsewhere to visit the class and discuss how math is used in weather forecasting.

Data and Statistics

Grouping
Small groups

You'll Need
For each group:
◆ Forecast Lineup (reproducible page 44)
◆ Pencils

Teaching Tip
If you have a large class or few local TV stations, assign two groups per station. One group can graph the high temperatures and the other can graph the low temperatures.

Writing Connection
Have students write letters to the winning station congratulating the weather forecasters on their "achievement" and explaining how the accuracy of their forecasts was determined.

Forecast Lineup

WEATHER FORECAST DATA FOR CHANNEL _____

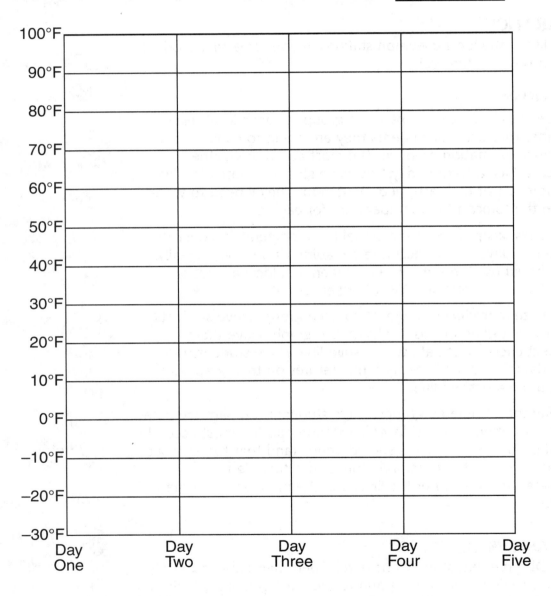

Temperature in Degrees Fahrenheit (°F)

100°F
90°F
80°F
70°F
60°F
50°F
40°F
30°F
20°F
10°F
0°F
–10°F
–20°F
–30°F

Day One   Day Two   Day Three   Day Four   Day Five

KEY

———————— = forecast temperature

– – – – – – = actual temperature

50+ Super-Fun Math Activities: Grade 6 © 2010 by Scholastic Inc.

Food for Thought

This activity will give students a "taste" of survey taking.

DIRECTIONS

1. Tell students that they are going to conduct a survey to find out more about the eating habits of the class. Hand out reproducible page 46, have each student fill it out, and collect the copies.

2. Have students tally the survey results. To save time, you may want to divide the class into groups and have each group tally a different question. Write the results for each question on the chalkboard.

3. Ask students how accurately they think the survey results would reflect the eating habits of all the sixth graders in your school. What about all the students in your town? All the sixth graders in the United States? In each case, ask students to suggest ways the accuracy of the survey could be improved.

 **ASSESSMENT**

Students should grasp that although the survey accurately reflects the eating habits of their own class and possibly of the sixth graders in your school, it would less accurately describe the eating habits of the entire school or of the population of sixth graders across the U.S. They should understand the reasoning behind that fact—differences in regional tastes might change the responses received.

➡➡➡ EXTENSION

Give students a choice of three types of graphs—bar, line, and circle—and ask them to decide what type of graph they would use to display the data in each question. (A circle graph would be best for questions with a finite number of choices, such as 3 and 5, while a bar graph would be better for more open-ended questions like 2 and 4. A line graph would work for question 10, since it measures the change in ice-cream eating habits of students over the course of a year.) Have groups of students take a question and actually create their choice of graph.

Grouping

Individual or whole class

 ## You'll Need

For each student:
◆ **Food for Thought (reproducible page 46)**
◆ Pencil

Name _____

Food for Thought

1. My favorite food is _____.

2. My least favorite food is _____.

3. Of these kinds of foods, the one I like best is (check only one):

☐ Italian   ☐ French

☐ Chinese   ☐ Mexican

☐ Japanese

4. The best food I ever ate was _____.

5. I eat at a fast-food restaurant (check only one):

☐ two or more times a week   ☐ once a month

☐ once a week   ☐ less than once a month

☐ once every few weeks

6. If I could have one thing for dessert, it would be (check one):

☐ Cake   ☐ Pie   ☐ Candy   ☐ Cookies

☐ Ice cream   ☐ Pudding   ☐ Fruit   ☐ Yogurt

☐ Other _____

7. When I come home from school, I (check only one):

☐ have a snack   ☐ do not have a snack

8. My favorite meal is (check only one):

☐ breakfast   ☐ lunch   ☐ dinner

9. I eat about _____ peanut butter and jelly sandwiches a month.

10. During one year, I eat ice cream about (fill in all the blanks):

_____ times in the winter   _____ times in the spring

_____ times in the summer   _____ times in the fall

Collect All Six

*"Six NBA glasses—collect the whole set!" Probability
shows students why that's easier said than done.*

DIRECTIONS

1. Distribute reproducible page 48. Then pose this situation to the class:

> Suppose a fast-food restaurant is giving away a free NBA All-Star glass with the purchase of a large soft drink. There are six glasses in the collection. When you buy your drink, you never know which glass you're going to receive.

Ask students to predict how many soft drinks they'd have to buy to get all six glasses. Have them write their prediction where indicated.

2. Explain to students that in this activity, the six numbers on the number cube will represent the six different NBA All-Star glasses. Each toss of the number cube represents the glass the student would receive. If a student rolls a two, for example, he or she would receive glass number two.

3. Have students toss the number cube and make a tally mark in the table in the Trial 1 row under the number rolled. Students should keep tossing the number cube and marking the results in the table. Trial 1 is over when every number on the cube has been rolled at least once. When students have finished Trial 1, have them record the total number of rolls in the trial.

4. Have students do nine more trials, each time keeping a tally of the number of rolls and recording the total number of rolls. When they've finished, have them compute the average of the total number of rolls for all ten trials and write the average where indicated on the recording sheet.

5. As a class, find the average of all the individual averages. Have students write that number where indicated on the recording sheet. Ask students to discuss what they learned. When they get glasses randomly, what can they say about their chances of getting a complete set?

ASSESSMENT

Students should understand that the final average represents a good idea of the number of soft drinks they'd have to buy to get all six NBA All-Star glasses, assuming all are equally available.

Grouping

Individual

You'll Need

For each student:

◆ **Collect All Six (reproducible page 48)**

◆ Number cube labeled 1–6

◆ Pencil

Writing Connection

Ask students to compare the final class average to the prediction they made at the beginning of the activity. Were there differences in the two numbers? Why or why not?

Collect All Six

How many soft drinks would you have to buy to get all six glasses?

My prediction: _____

Now roll your number cube. Make a tally mark under the number you get. For each Trial, keep rolling until you get all six numbers. Then count up the total number of rolls for that Trial. Complete all 10 Trials.

Number Rolled	1	2	3	4	5	6	Total Number of Rolls
Trial 1							
Trial 2							
Trial 3							
Trial 4							
Trial 5							
Trial 6							
Trial 7							
Trial 8							
Trial 9							
Trial 10							

Average number of times rolled in one trial—ME: _____

Average number of times rolled in one trial—MY CLASS: _____

True Colors

Students show their school spirit with colors and combinations.

DIRECTIONS

1. Pose the following problem: You and some friends want to come to school dressed in the school's colors, color A and color B. (Substitute your own school's colors here.) Each person will wear one color or the other. In a group of five students, for example, all five group members might choose to wear color A, or four members might wear color A while one wears color B. How many different combinations of students and colors can you make?

2. Assign students to groups of three, four, five, and six. (Make sure there is at least one group of each number). Challenge each group to solve the problem using the number of students in their group. Encourage the group members to use any solution method they'd like—some may want to act out the problem, while others may wish to draw a diagram.

3. When the groups have finished, have a student from each group give their answer and explain their solution method. If groups with the same number of members do not have the same answer, discuss the results with the class to determine which answer is correct.

ASSESSMENT

Listen as students describe their problem-solving strategies. Note if students are able to devise a way to keep track of their combinations so they are not counting the same ones, or missing any possibilities.

Answers: 3 students can create 8 combinations, as follows:

◆ 1 combination of three students wearing color A

◆ 3 combinations of two students wearing color A and one wearing color B

◆ 3 combinations of one student wearing color A and two wearing color B

◆ 1 combination of three students wearing color B

For 4 students, 16 combinations; 5 students, 32 combinations; 6 students, 64 combinations.

Grouping
Small groups

You'll Need
◆ Paper
◆ Crayons of two different colors

Teaching Tip

If students have trouble conceptualizing who in their group is wearing each color, have them create models out of construction paper.

Grouping

Whole class

You'll Need

◆ 2 coins

Teaching Tip

If you don't have time for 50 coin tosses, you can reduce the number, but be sure to do at least 20 pairs of tosses.

Writing Connection

Explain that the result is a mathematical probability and that other factors may skew that probability. For example, the odds would be skewed if the teams were a minor league team and a major league team. Have students make a list of other factors that might skew the probability for the case of baseball games.

Probability Doubleheader

What are a team's chances of winning at least one game of a doubleheader? Probability can help students figure it out!

PREPARATION

Before class, copy this chart on the chalkboard or overhead.

Team Wins Game A and/or Game B	Team Loses Game A and B

DIRECTIONS

1. Ask students to imagine that their favorite baseball team is playing a doubleheader: two games. What is the probability that the team will win at least one game of the doubleheader? Encourage students to discuss their opinions.

2. Show students the two coins. Tell them that coin A will represent the first game of the doubleheader, Game A. Coin B will represent the second game of the doubleheader, Game B. Coin tosses will represent wins and losses.

3. Ask a student to toss coin A. If the coin lands heads up, it represents a win in Game A. If it lands tails up, it represents a loss. Then have another student toss coin B. If it lands heads up, the team wins Game B. If it lands tails up, the team loses Game B. After both coins have been tossed, make a tally mark in the chart under the column that describes the results of the two tosses. Did the team win at least one game? (Tally in Column 1.) Or did the team lose both games? (Tally in Column 2.)

4. Have students do 49 additional tosses of coin A and coin B. After each, make a tally mark to show the results of the pair of tosses.

5. After 50 pairs of tosses, add the number of tally marks in each column. Have students write a ratio that compares the number in Column 1 to the total number of pairs of tosses (in this case, 50). Writing this ratio as a percent, they'll express the probability the team will win at least one of the two games of the doubleheader.

ASSESSMENT

Students may assume that the chances of the baseball team winning at least one game is 50 percent, since the chances of winning either game is 50 percent. By doing the activity, they should see that the chances are actually about 75 percent.

Boning Up on Ratios

Students use ratio and proportion to estimate a person's height based on the length of a single bone.

DIRECTIONS

1. Ask students to imagine that they've found a human lower leg bone that's several thousand years old. Is there a way they could use it to determine how tall the person was? Allow students to discuss their ideas.

2. Have students pair up. Each student should find the length, in centimeters, of his or her lower leg (from the ankle to the knee) and his or her height (from head to toe). Have students round each measurement to the nearest centimeter.

3. Students can use the measurements to write a ratio that compares the two lengths. Remind them to write their ratios in lowest terms.

4. Have students determine how close their own ratio of leg length to height is to their partner's ratio. One way to do that is by setting up a proportion and cross-multiplying:

$$\frac{\text{Student A's lower leg length}}{\text{Student A's height}} \overset{?}{=} \frac{\text{Student B's lower leg length}}{\text{Student B's height}}$$

5. The proportions will rarely be exact; however, by having pairs compare their results with other pairs, students will see they're close. As a class, use the findings to decide whether or not they could use this ratio to determine the height of a person if they know the length of the lower leg bone.

ASSESSMENT

Observe whether students are recording measurements accurately and setting up their proportions correctly. If any pair's proportions vary widely from the rest of the class, ask the class to check their work.

⟩⟩⟩ EXTENSION

Have the class find ratios that compare other parts of their bodies: arm to hand, head to height, and so on. They should determine if the proportions hold for many cases by pooling their information.

 Grouping

Pairs

 You'll Need

For each pair:
◆ Centimeter tape measures
◆ Paper
◆ Pencils

 Teaching Tip

If centimeter tape measures aren't available, have students measure body parts with string, then measure each length of string with a centimeter ruler.

 Writing Connection

Ask students to explain how one of these professionals might use the information they've just discovered: archaeologist, police officer, doctor, physical therapist.

Shopping Abroad

Students take a shopping "trip" to see what an item of their choice would cost in other currencies.

Grouping

Individual

You'll Need

◆ **Shopping Abroad (reproducible page 53),** one copy for each student

◆ Catalogs featuring clothing, electronics, or other items of interest to students

◆ Foreign currency equivalents chart (newspaper financial section or online)

◆ Pencils

Writing Connection

Have students write a story about traveling to one of the countries listed in the reproducible. They should include mention of the country's monetary unit in their story.

DIRECTIONS

1. Invite students to shop, with this stipulation—they'll "spend" currency from another country. Distribute the catalogs. Ask students to pick out one item they want to buy, and write down the item and its price.

2. Explain that while people in the U.S. use dollars as their main unit of money, people in other countries use different units with different values. Using ratios and percents, students can see how dollars and various foreign money units relate to one another.

3. Hand out reproducible page 53. As a class, fill in the Ratio of U.S. dollar to currency column by using the newspaper or online source to find the current values of each currency listed. Make sure students express each value as a ratio of one dollar to the other currency's exchange.

4. Have students find the amount they'd have to pay to purchase their item in each currency by setting up and solving proportions. For example, if the ratio of a dollar to a Polish zloty is 1 to 2.8 and a student's item costs $15.99, he or she could set up the proportion shown at right.

$$\frac{1}{2.8} = \frac{15.99}{x}$$

By solving for x and rounding to the nearest hundredth, students find they'd spend 44.77 zlotys to buy the item in Poland. As students find the value of the item in each currency, have them record the value on the reproducible.

5. Have students compare findings and discuss the results. Although each student has chosen a different item to buy, the cost in any currency is proportional. Students may be surprised at how many units of another currency it takes to buy the items of their choice.

➡➡➡ EXTENSION

Using an almanac or other research, have students find the average annual value of the currencies listed in the Shopping Abroad reproducible over the past several years. Then have them graph the values by year and determine which currency has experienced the most fluctuation.

Name _____

Shopping Abroad

Item I'll buy _____

Cost in U.S. dollars _____

FOREIGN CURRENCY VALUES AS OF _____
(DATE)

Country	Name of currency	Ratio of U.S. dollar to currency	Cost of my item
China	renminbi		
France	euro		
Ghana	cedi		
India	rupee		
Israel	shekel		
Japan	yen		
Norway	krone		
Poland	zloty		
Russia	ruble		
United Kingdom	pound		

Grandma's Muffins

Does Grandma have enough raisins to bake her muffins? It's up to students—and percents—to decide!

Grouping

Small groups

You'll Need

For each group:

◆ 12-ounce box of raisin bran

◆ Scale

◆ Two containers for separating cereal and raisins

Teaching Tip

If you don't have enough cereal boxes and/or scales for all the small groups, you can do this activity as a class.

DIRECTIONS

1. Introduce the problem: Grandma is making her famous chock full o' raisins muffins for the town bake sale. But she's out of raisins! What she does have is raisin bran—three 12-ounce boxes. She decides to pick the raisins out of the cereal and use them in the muffins. The recipe calls for 2 pounds of raisins. Will the raisins in the cereal boxes be enough?

2. Have students offer suggestions about how they might solve the problem. Then ask them if it would be helpful to know the percentage of the cereal's weight that was made of raisins. How could they find the percentage?

3. Divide the class into groups of four or five. Provide each group with one box of cereal and a scale and have them try to solve the problem. Then discuss their findings. How did they find out if Grandma's three boxes of cereal would yield the 2 pounds of raisins she needed? Was it necessary to separate all the cereal and raisins to find out?

ASSESSMENT

The key to solving this problem is finding out what percent of the weight of the cereal the raisins comprise. Students should see that once they've estimated the weight of the raisins in one box of cereal, it is easy to determine whether three boxes of cereal will provide the correct amount of raisins.

➤➤➤ EXTENSIONS

◆ Have students apply the idea of percent of weight to explain how they would solve the Grandma's muffins problem with different sizes of cereal boxes, a 9-ounce box, for example.

◆ Have students check the percentage weight of raisins in different brands of raisin bran. Is one brand a clear winner in having a higher percentage of its weight comprised of raisins?

The World's Corniest Riddle

Students work with coordinate points to solve a riddle that's all "ears"!

DIRECTIONS

1. Tell students they'll be locating points on a grid to solve a riddle. Review the concept of coordinate graphing with students. Make sure they understand that:

   ◆ in an ordered pair of numbers, the first number represents a point along the x-axis, and the second number represents a point along the y-axis.

   ◆ if a number in an ordered pair is negative, you move to the left on the x-axis or down on the y-axis. If the number is positive, you move to the right on the x-axis or up on the y-axis.

2. Distribute reproducible page 56 and have students complete it.

ASSESSMENT

Students should get the following solution: *It goes in one ear and out the other.* If they do not, review which axis each number in an ordered pair represents and which direction they should be traveling on each axis.

▶▶▶ EXTENSION

Distribute graph paper and have students make up their own riddles and answers using a coordinate grid like the one in the reproducible. They can exchange and solve each other's riddles.

✦✦✦ VARIATION

Use masking tape to make a four-quadrant grid on your classroom floor. Have students locate the placement of their desks as coordinates on the grid.

Grouping

Individual

You'll Need

For each student:

◆ **The World's Corniest Riddle (reproducible page 56)**

◆ Pencil

The World's Corniest Riddle

You have never heard a riddle as corny as this one! You'll find the answer to the riddle in this coordinate grid. Each blank below has an ordered pair of numbers under it. Match each pair with a point on the grid. Write the letter of that point in the blank.

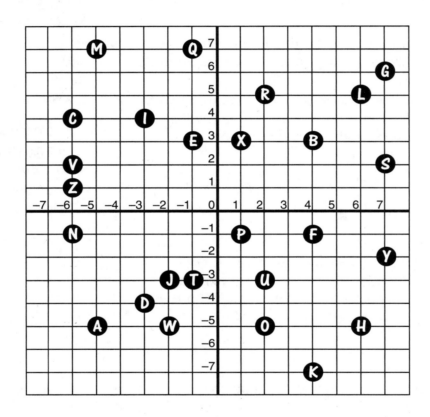

WHAT DOES A FRUIT FLY DO IN A CORNFIELD?

___ ___ ___ ___ ___ ___ ___ ___ ___ ___ ___
(−3,4) (−1,−3) (7,6) (2,−5) (−1,3) (7,2) (−3,4) (−6,−1) (2,−5) (−6,−1) (−1,3)

___ ___ ___ ___ ___ ___ ___ ___ ___
(−1,3) (−5,−5) (2,5) (−5,−5) (−6,−1) (−3,−4) (2,−5) (2,−3) (−1,−3)

                                                    !

___ ___ ___ ___ ___ ___ ___ ___
(−1,−3) (6,−5) (−1,3) (2,−5) (−1,−3) (6,−5) (−1,3) (2,5)

50+ Super-Fun Math Activities: Grade 6 © 2010 by Scholastic Inc.

What's Your Function?

Tallyho! Students gather data, create tables, and graph results to understand algebraic functions.

DIRECTIONS

1. Divide the class into groups of five or six. Have them each number a paper from 1 to 5, and then answer these questions:

   1. How many ears do you have?
   2. How many brothers and sisters do you have?
   3. How many days per week do you go to school?
   4. How many pets do you have?
   5. How many fingers do you have?

2. Ask each group to make a running tally for the data in each question. Each tally should start with one group member's response and then add on responses from other members, each time adding the cumulative responses. The data and tally for one group's answers to the fourth question might look like this:

3. After each group has made a count for each question, have group members look for a pattern in each set. What do the questions whose answers form patterns have in common?

4. Ask students what might happen if they graphed each tally on a coordinate grid. What would the graph for each tally look like? Have students test their ideas by marking coordinates on their grid paper and graphing the data.

 ASSESSMENT

Students should recognize that the data for the first and last questions form a pattern, because each student will answer the question in the same way. In the first question, the numbers will always increase by 2; in the last, by 5. Question 3 will most likely increase by 5. Each of these sets of data are functions: the data follow a rule of correspondence. Questions 2 and 4 may or may not be functions, depending on the students.

VARIATION

You can substitute other types of data for your questions. Make sure two or three of the questions will produce responses that are functional relationships. For example, a car drives 50 miles each hour; a student earns $1.50 each hour. Ask students to suggest data that are related in this way.

 Grouping

Small groups

You'll Need

◆ Paper
◆ Pencils
◆ Grid paper

	Number of pets	Total pets in group
Leilani	2	2
Andrew	4	6
Jill	2	8
Carol	2	10
Tyrone	0	10

Tip or Balance?

Students create and experiment with simple equations.

PREPARATION

Draw a simple diagram of a pan balance on the chalkboard.

DIRECTIONS

1. Tell students they'll use the idea of a two-pan balance with numbers. Review the signs > (greater than) and < (less than). Then write these number sentences in the left and right sides of the scale: 3 x 7 + 6; 3 x 9. Will the scale balance? If not, which symbol, > or <, will make the statement true? Do the activity again with the following pairs of number sentences:

   4 + 25 − 6; 3 x 7   6 x 7; (3 + 2) x 8

   Ask volunteers which signs would make the statements true. Ask others to explain what could be done to either number sentence to make the scale balance.

2. Challenge students to write two expressions for each side of the scale that will make it balance. After a few minutes, ask them to share their expressions. Have the class test each one.

3. Now add the idea of using variables in the two-pan balance. Write these expressions in the left and right sides of the scale:

   3 x ◯ + ☐; 2 x ☐ − 4

   Ask students to find numbers that can be substituted for the circle and square to make the scale balance. If calculators are available, students might use them to try their ideas more quickly.

ASSESSMENT

This activity will help students develop appropriate meanings for equality and variables as a readiness for algebra.

▶▶▶ **EXTENSION**

Add to students' understanding of equations by asking them to draw a balanced scale, put in expressions on either side that make it balance, and then try these:

◆ Subtract 3 from each side. What happens?

◆ Multiply each side by 5. What happens?

◆ Add 100 to each side. What happens?

PAN BALANCE

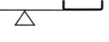

Name _____

Problems and More

Put on your thinking caps to solve these problems.

1. A REAL PAGE TURNER

Secret agent Mattie Harry has been captured by the evil Dr. Sebastian. He wants her to tell where she's hidden the secret brain-booster formula.

Finally, Mattie gives in. "It's written on a piece of paper that's hidden in my code book," she says. "I put it between pages 169 and 170."

Dr. Sebastian rushes off to check, and Mattie escapes. Was she telling the truth? Will Dr. Sebastian find the secret formula? (Hint: Look at pages 169 and 170 in several books.)

_____

2. SQUARE ROOTS

In the design below, how many squares contain an even number of flowers? (Hint: First, find all the squares.)

3. TAKE YOUR PICK

You've just won the House 'n' Home Sweepstakes. You can take your prize in either of two ways. Plan A: You can take $10,000 every day for 30 days. Plan B: You can take one cent on the first day, double that amount the next day, double that amount the next day, and so on for 30 days. Which way would you choose? Why?

_____

4. TRICKY TRIANGLES

How can you create four triangles using only six toothpicks? Try it.
(Hint: Think 3-D!)

5. ROUNDABOUT SMILE

Suppose you roll the face on the left all the way around the face on the right. Will the face be right side up or upside down?

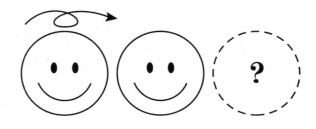

Problems and More

6. PRODUCTIVE MAZE

Find your way through the maze below. Draw a path from the Start box to the Finish box so that the product of the numbers along the path equals the number in the Finish box. You can move up, down, or across, but not diagonally. You don't have to enter every box, but you can't enter a box more than once.

Start 7	2	4
8	3	5
1	6	Finish 5,040

7. $100 DART

At the amusement park, you get six darts to throw at these targets. If you score a total of 100, you win $100.00. You can hit each target as many times as you wish. In which targets do you want the six darts to go?

   (24) (17) (23) (39) (16)

8. STATE OF MIND

What state contains $\frac{1}{4}$ of Nebraska, $\frac{3}{5}$ of Whale, $\frac{1}{3}$ of Jam, $\frac{1}{3}$ of Lampshade, and $\frac{3}{3}$ of Ire? (Hint: Look carefully at the letters!)

_____

9. IT'S ABOUT TIME!

The equations below don't work. But adding a label to each number can make each one true. What labels could you add? (Hint: The labels in each equation are different words.)

$$1 - 23 = 60$$
$$1 - 24 = 1$$
$$1 - 16 = 1$$

10. PATTERN SQUARES

Count the squares in each figure. Write the numbers for the next four figures.

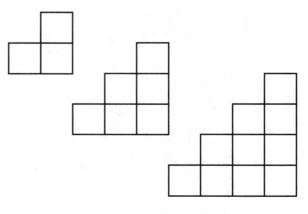

_____, _____, _____, _____

50+ Super-Fun Math Activities: Grade 6 © 2010 by Scholastic Inc.

Answers on page 64.

An Assessment Toolkit

Alternative methods of assessment provide a comprehensive profile for each student. As students work on *50+ Super-Fun Math Activities: Grade 6*, here are some ways you might observe and record their work. Alone or in combination, they can provide a quick snapshot that will add to your knowledge of students' development in mathematics. They also give you concrete observations to share with families at reporting time.

FILE CARDS

An alphabetical file system, with a card for each student, provides a handy way to keep notes on students' progress. Choose a few students each day that you plan to observe. Pull their cards, jot down the date and activity, and record comments about their work.

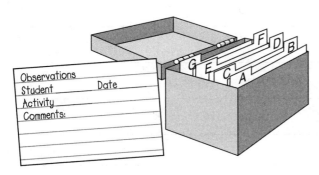

CLIPBOARDS

With a list of students attached to your clipboard, you can easily move about the classroom and jot down observations about their work and their thinking. If you want to focus on a particular skill or competency, you can create a quick checklist and simply check as you observe.

STICKY NOTES

As you circulate while individuals or small groups are working, create a sticky note for students who show particular strengths or areas for your attention and help. Be sure to date the note. The advantage to this technique is that you can move the notes to a record folder to create a profile; you can also cluster students with similar competencies as a reminder for later grouping.

CHECKLISTS AND RUBRICS

On pages 62 and 63, you'll find a few ready-made checklists and a rubric. Feel free to modify them to suit your own needs. Invite students to assess their own work—they are honest and insightful, and you'll have another perspective on their mathematical development!

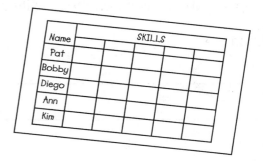

Self-Evaluation Form

ACTIVITY _____

1. The activity was **(HARD EASY)** to complete because _____

_____

_____

2. The part of the activity I did best was _____

_____

_____

3. I could have done a better job if _____

_____

_____

4. The mathematics I used was _____

_____

_____

5. After completing the activity I felt _____

because _____

_____

_____

6. I would rate my work on the activity as **(EXCELLENT GOOD FAIR POOR)**

because _____

_____

50+ Super-Fun Math Activities: Grade 6 © 2010 by Scholastic Inc.

Assessment Checklist

Activity _____ Date _____ Group _____

Students					
MATHEMATICS KNOWLEDGE					
Understands problem or task					
Formulates and carries out a plan					
Explains concepts clearly					
Uses models or tools appropriately					
Makes connections to similar problems					
Can create similar problems					
MATHEMATICAL PROCESSES					
Justifies responses logically					
Listens carefully to others and evaluates information					
Reflects on and explains procedures					
LEARNING DISPOSITIONS					
Tackles difficult tasks					
Perseveres					
Shows confidence in own ability					
Collaborates/shares ideas					

SCORING RUBRIC

3 Fully accomplishes the task

Shows full understanding of the central mathematical idea(s)

Communicates thinking clearly using oral explanation or written, symbolic, or visual means

2 Partially accomplishes the task

Shows partial understanding of the central mathematical idea(s)

Written or oral explanation partially communicates thinking, but may be incomplete, misdirected, or not clearly presented

1 Does not accomplish the task

Shows little or no grasp of the central mathematical idea(s)

Recorded work or oral explanation is fragmented and not understandable

Answers to Problems and More

PAGES 40-41

1. Possible answers: add any number between 47 and 146; subtract any number between 854 and 953.

2.
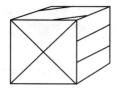

3. Two possible answers:
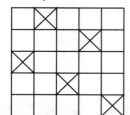 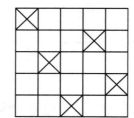

4.
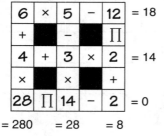

5. The sum is always 65.

6. 27 matches

7. 6 cowboys and 11 cows

8. The bottom cog will turn to the right.

9.
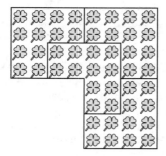

10. He needs to get 97.

PAGES 59-60

1. Mattie is not telling the truth. Pages 169 and 170 of any book are back-to-back pages, so nothing could be stored between them.

2. Twenty squares contain an even number of flowers.

3. You should take plan B. With plan A, you would have $300,000 on day 30. With plan B, you would have $5,368,709 and change on day 30.

4. You can build a triangular pyramid. The four triangles are the three faces and the base of the pyramid.

5. The face will be right side up.

6. You should travel through the 7, 2, 4, 5, 3, and 6 squares.

7. Four darts should hit the 17 target; two darts should hit the 16 target.

8. New Hampshire

9. 1 day − 23 hours = 60 minutes
   1 yard − 24 inches = 1 foot
   1 quart − 16 ounces = 1 pint

10. The next four numbers in the pattern are 15, 21, 28, 36.